The Tales of Jamison Sheblis
The Lost Puppy

Written by Suzanne Ellen

Illustrated in collaboration with AI, guided by the heart of Jamison Sheblis

Published & Powered by
S. E. Shore Corp

Squan Beach, NJ

Copyright © 2025 Suzanne Ellen

All rights reserved. No part of this publication may be reproduced, stored in a retrieval system, or transmitted in any form or by any means—electronic, mechanical, photocopying, recording, or otherwise—without prior written permission from the publisher.

Written by Suzanne Ellen

Illustrated in collaboration with AI,
guided by the heart of Jamison herself

Published & Powered by S. E. Shore Corp
First edition, 2025

Inspired by the true story of Jamison Sheblis,
who rescued us as much as we rescued her.

For every soul who's ever been lost,
and every heart brave enough to find them.

ISBN 978-1-80623-353-3

Certificate of Adoption

for

Jamison Sheblis

Name _____

Date _____

Signature _____

There once was a puppy,
abandoned and small,
on the shores of Squan, with no
one to call.

Afraid of the ocean,
with her furry wet paws,
she chased after seagulls
and ran without pause.

Past the big houses,
she darted in fright,
from beach to the sidewalk,
then out of plain sight.

Towards the town sign, she looked all around. "Oh, what will I see?"

Passing a lagoon
and boats,
she ran free,
searching high
and low
for her family.

Down into town,
on Main Street she sped,
where Veterans marched
with flags overhead.

With medals and pets, and the puppy watched
they paraded with pride, from the road at their side.

Now it was night,
and the stars had all shone.
How scraggly and hungry
she'd quietly grown.

No family in sight,
no place to call home—
the poor little puppy
was all alone.

At the break of day,
the dog catcher came,
and carried her off
with no tag and no name.

She watched the beach town
fade soft and serene—
like a whispering wave,
like a long-lost dream.

She stayed in a cage,
as sad as can be

Wondering if someone
will ever love me

"I hope one of them notices little ol' me…"

She smiled, waved her paw, and wagged happily.

"Look—I'm over here! They call me Shelby!"

They stopped and they played,
then I was alone,
They smiled and they waved
as they headed home.

Still in the cage tagged 'Shelby,'
I whispered soft and low:
'All I want is love and care—
a place to call my own.'

'All i want is love
and a fur-ever home.

Weeks had gone by,
I kept waiting to see
if someone would come
to rescue me...

... and my furry baby,
tucked close at my side,
the secret I carried,
too quiet to hide,
with tears in my eyes.

One week before Christmas,
they left through the door.

A forever home,
she'd wait for no more.

As they snuggled by the tree, Suzanna Claws said, "How about we name you Jamison Sheblis?"

COLORING PAGE
MEET JAMISON SHEBLIS

Write About Jamison Sheblis

How did Jamison Sheblis's story make you feel? Draw or write about a time you felt brave, lost, or found something special.

Positive Paw-situdes!

- I am brave
- I am loved
- I am strong
- I am not alone
- I am important
- I can do hard things

Trace Jamison's Journey
✦ A Follow-the-Dots Adventure ✦

Help Jamison Sheblis Find Her Way Home!

Meet the Real Jamison Sheblis

In real life. Jamison Sheblis was more than a lost puppy—she was a brave little soul with a big heart and an even bigger journey ahead.

Abandoned and found wandering the beach, Jamison was rescued and brought to safety by kind hands. Not long after, she met her forever family—and everything changed.

With her gentle eyes and loyal spirit, Jamison became a beloved companion, emotional support pup, and the inspiration for this entire series.

Through each turn of the page, her story lives on... reminding us that sometimes, the ones who are lost are the ones who help us find our way. ♥

Thank You

for reading Jamison Sheblis's story.

Every time her tale is shared, her heart lives on.

The Tales of Jamison Sheblis...

New friends to meet,
new places to roam—
From bayou streets
to a Texas home.

With love and courage,
she'll never be alone...
Jamison's journey
has just begun to be known.

bonus page

Don't forget to tell Jamison Sheblis and Aunt Suzanna which part you liked best, and why!

Write your message below, in words or pictures.

www.ingramcontent.com/pod-product-compliance
Lightning Source LLC
Chambersburg PA
CBHW061146070526
44584CB00033B/4438